HAWAII TO DA MAX

Conceived and written by
DOUGLAS SIMONSON
KEN SAKATA
PAT SASAKI

With a Special Mahalo to
STUART W. LESSES

Illustrated by
DOUGLAS SIMONSON
ANGIE ACAIN
TODD KUROSAWA

Designed by
PAUL S. OTAGURO

Published by
PEPPOVISION
222 S. Vineyard St., Suite 501
Honolulu, Hawaii 96813

Copyright 1983 Peppovision, Inc.
All Rights Reserved

Printed in the United States of America

A WORD FROM THE AUTHORS

We would like to say Mahalo e Aloha to all the people who supported our first book, PIDGIN TO DA MAX. Their inspiration has made it possible for us to continue expressing our aloha, humor and ideas in exciting new ways. We welcome you to be part of it. "No make shame, e komo mai!"

HAWAII TO DA MAX is our way of saying Aloha—or "Howzit!"—to all of you who are visiting the Hawaiian Islands. The coming together of people and cultures from all over the world is an important part of the magic of Hawaii. You, too, are part of this.

It is our intention to help you understand and relate to locals (don't call us "natives") so that your stay here is that much more enjoyable, rewarding and FUN. This book is meant to give you a better chance to really communicate with the people here, and make your memories that much richer when you get back home.

Mahalo nui loa,

Doug
Ken
Pat

P.S. This is our friend Ipo (EE po) — Hawaiian for "sweetheart" — a Hawaiian menehune who will be appearing in various parts of this book to guide you and give you a laugh. Like all menehunes (meh neh HOO nays), Ipo appears in strange places and disappears for no apparent reason. But when he's around he always makes us feel good.

CLOSING THOUGHTS

**If you've read this book,
Hawaii is already in your heart
. . . just look!**

JUST IN CASE you'd like additional copies of HAWAII TO DA MAX, we've supplied an order blank.

We'd like to hear from you, too—tell us what you liked or didn't like about HAWAII TO DA MAX, and if you have suggestions for changes or additions, we'd like to hear them.

Comments: _____
_____
_____
_____
_____
_____
_____
_____

We'd also like to invite you to order a copy or two of our local guide to Pidgin, PIDGIN TO DA MAX, a 112-page Pidgin dictionary illustrated with cartoons. Also available is Volume II of PIDGIN TO DA MAX, entitled PIDGIN TO DA MAX HANA HOU.

Please send me _____ copy(s) of HAWAII TO DA MAX @ $4.00 each.

TOTAL $_____

Please send me _____ copy(s) of PIDGIN TO DA MAX @ $5.50 each.

TOTAL $_____

Please send me _____ copy(s) of PIDGIN TO DA MAX HANA HOU @ $5.50 each.

TOTAL $_____

I enclose my check or money order (payable to PEPPOVISION, INC.) in the total amount of $_____.

NAME _____

ADDRESS _____

_____ ZIP _____

(Prices include tax, shipping and handling. Please allow 4-6 weeks for delivery.)

MAHALO
(ma HA lo)
Means "T'anks eh?" Used mostly by entertainers, aunties, and inter-island flight attendants.

ACKNOWLEDGEMENTS

Graphic Prep, Inc.
Harris & Smith, Attys.
Hawaii Travel Industry
Hawaii Visitors Bureau
Kent Ishibashi
Victoria Lam
Nelson and Elvira Lee
Stuart Lesses
Kregg Luke

M-P Partners
Wayne Miyaji
Pioneer Plaza Club
Sanoe Enterprises
Barbara Tong
Tongg Publishing Co.
Trans National Travel
Terry Wong, CPA
Westwind Travel

CREDITS: Design, Douglas Simonson and Paul Otaguro; Layout, Paul Otaguro; Printing, Tongg Printing; Typesetting and Photography, Graphic Prep, Inc.

All characters in HAWAII TO DA MAX are fictional. Any resemblance to real people, living or dead, is coincidental. No part of this book may be reproduced in any form without permission in writing from the publisher.

Embrace the fire; return to mountain.

DECEMBER/KEKEMAPA

25 CHRISTMAS IN HAWAII

Skiing on the slopes of Mauna Kea on the Big Island; Christmas Tree Festival at NBC (Neal Blaisdell Center) and City Hall; students returning home from the Mainland; visitors from everywhere coming to share in the Hawaiian weather; handmade Christmas angels of coconut husk, haole koa seeds and other local materials; a Santa Claus with red shorts and a surfboard; trans-Pacific telephone marathon; long lines at the Post Office; pupu parties at the office, park or beach; Christmas trees arriving from the Mainland; singing "Mele Kalikimaka"; hearing "Silent Night" sung in Hawaiian; midnight services at Kawaiahao Church.

31 NEW YEAR'S EVE

Time to say aloha to the old year, tell your friends you not going be kolohe (rascal) anymore; bust out the boxes and boxes of fireworks and firecrackers you've been saving up; clean the house; pound mochi (rice cake) for eating and for good luck; pay off all your bills; comfort the poor dog who has to suffer through all the noise and smoke of New Year's Eve in Hawaii; and okole maluna (bottoms up!) with a New Year's toast. But no drink too much — we like see you around next year, yeah? Hauoli Makahiki Hou means HAPPY NEW YEAR!!

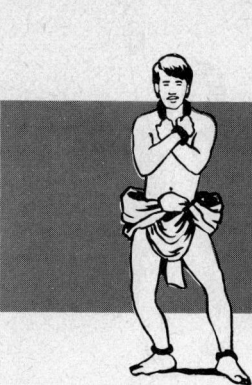

Follow closely;
the clouds pass quietly.

NOVEMBER/NOWEMAPA

FALL/WINTER SEASON CONTINUED
Hints of holiday fever, Veterans Day, General Election. Bust out the long pants for chilly evenings, or whip on your baggies (surfer shorts) and surfboard and head for the North Shore — but only if you're a good surfer. Big winter swells coming!

Breathe deeply;
the sweet rains have come.

OCTOBER/OKAKOPA

DISCOVERERS' DAY
Hawaii's discoverer (the first non-Polynesian, anyway) was Captain James Cook, who landed on the beach of Kealakekua Bay on the Big Island in 1778. (Our Hawaiian Bicentennial celebration was held in 1978.) Cook's discovery is recognized as the official beginning of dramatic changes in Hawaiian history — the introduction of Western philosophies and international contact for the Islands.

she carries the sea and sky.

SEPTEMBER/KEPAKEMAPA

LABOR DAY WEEKEND/BACK TO SCHOOL DAZE
For the mainland-bound students, it's not only Aloha to summer but Aloha to LOCAL KINE STUFFS — like standard dress: t-shirts, shorts and rubber slippers; smells of the ocean and flowers; always green mountains to see; rice and shoyu with almost everything, not to mention plate lunches and saimin; sounds of pidgin; sunshine all year round. The school year means "care packages" for mainland students, filled with Hawaii-only stuffs like crack seed, mochi crunch, small rice cooker, instant saimin, a Makaha Sons of Niihau or Brothers Cazimero or Melveen Leed record album, and copies of Pidgin to da Max!

FALL/WINTER SEASON
Aloha Week Parade and Court, Iron Man Competition (Big Island version of the Triathlon), Honolulu Marathon (one of the biggest anywhere!), more crafts fairs including the annual Kupuna Festival, start of the Honolulu Symphony Season which runs from September through April, surfing meets (big surf starts soon), and lots more. Also time for local people to start preparing for wintertime when nighttime temperatures sometimes drop to below 60 degrees — we have to put on our long pants!

PRIMARY ELECTION DAY
When you can see electioneers standing on street corners in aloha shirts and wearing leis and a big Hawaiian smile, giving the "shaka" sign, hoping you'll remember their candidate!

Taste the mist;

AUGUST/AUKAKE

21 ADMISSIONS DAY
When we celebrate becoming a State. Young and beautiful, this 50th State, with much aloha for the other 49!

PLUM SEASON
Kokee on Kauai is known for its small but very sweet plums; it's a short season so wiki-wiki (hurry) and appreciate them while you can!

SUMMER SEASON CONTINUED
Annual Transpacific Yacht Race (the Transpac) with local and international entries; Kona (Big Island) Billfish Tournament also brings friends from all over the world; last chance to sleep late before school begins; party, go beach, have picnics; time to say aloha to those returning to school on the mainland and aloha to those returning to Hawaii from the mainland.

her petals embrace the sun.

JULY/IULAI

4 INDEPENDENCE DAY
Remember, Hawaii is not a foreign country. We celebrate the 4th, too, with fireworks and picnics filled with the smell of Korean shortribs, teriyaki meats and so much more, cooked on the hibachi and served to ohana (family) and friends.

MANGO SEASON
Almost pau! Freeze 'em already.

SUMMER SEASON CONTINUED
Sandbuilding contest, Ye Olde World Faire at Hawaii Loa College on the Windward side, Annual Ukulele Festival at Kapiolani Parks Bandstand, Annual Hawaiian Music Festival (Kailua/Kaneohe), State Farm Fair, County Fairs. . .

PRINCE LOT HULA FESTIVAL
Named for Prince Lot, King Kamehameha V, last of the Kamehameha rulers, this festival is performed on the only known earth platform to be used exclusively for hula and dedicated during this century. The setting is lovely Moanalua Valley, with many large, spreading trees, a taro patch, carp pond, old homes once used by royalty, a running stream, and demonstrations of Hawaiian arts and crafts. For a taste of real Hawaiian celebration, don't miss this! But come early — plenny people going be there with their ice chests and straw mats to get a good place on the grass.

INTERARTS FESTIVAL Sponsored by the University of Hawaii, this is a showcase for multiethnic culture and arts from Hawaii's people, with music, dance, drama, visual arts and literature.
This runs through August so you'll have plenty of time to enjoy it. Come, okay?

Drink the warmth;

JUNE/IUNE

MANGO SEASON CONTINUED
Mango smoothies, mango cake, mango jam, mango jelly... eat now, pretty soon pau!

GRADUATION TIME!
Leis over the top of your head and draped over both arms... June is celebration for graduating seniors and it's real party time. Lots of school pride, too. In Hawaii we don't say "What's your sign?", we say "What school you grad from?"

SUMMER SEASON
So much to do and see and eat! What makes a Hawaiian summer? Try: shave ice with ice cream and azuki beans; fishing; diving; camping; hiking; sailing; laying crab net; getting a tan; outdoor crafts fairs; outrigger canoe races; Fiesta Filipina Festival; runners' race to the summit of Haleakala on the island of Maui; coffee season on the Big Island; local kids visiting aunties and uncles on the neighbor islands.

11 KAMEHAMEHA DAY
The Hawaiian chief who united our islands and became our King in the 18th century, starting the line of the ruling Kamehameha family. The Kam Day Parade is a must-see! Many couples have exchanged wedding vows at the foot of his statue, which is draped with hundreds of flower leis on this special day.

JAPANESE BON FESTIVAL
From late June through early August, Buddhist tradition honors those who have passed with Bon Dances. The evening events are filled with the sounds of drums and singing, lively dancing, bright kimonos and ono food! A stunning sight is the Lantern Festival in Haleiwa — hundreds of lanterns are set afloat to light the face of the ocean. Chicken skin!

Close your eyes;
the stream begins to flow.

MAY/MEI

1 MAY DAY
It's Lei Day in Hawaii, with lots happening: the selection of the Lei Queen and her court... pageants held at many elementary schools... lei making and display contests everywhere... and the May Day Concert by the Brothers Cazimero at the Waikiki Shell under the stars. It gets better every year — get your tickets early!

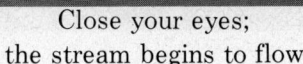

5 BOYS' DAY
Another easy one to remember — 5th day of the 5th month. You know it's coming when you see large, colorful cloth or paper carp (one for each son in the family) flying above Japanese homes. They must be proud, yeah?

MOTHERS DAY
Mothers in Hawaii are just like mothers everywhere — and we love them!

30 MEMORIAL DAY
This is the day we remember those who are no longer with us. Take a drive to Punchbowl National Cemetery where the Boy Scouts place flower leis on each gravesite. And at the Arizona Memorial, flower wreaths are tossed gently onto the waters of Pearl Harbor. Come and share in our Aloha!

MANGO SEASON
...means MANGOES to da max! Try eating mango right off the seed...juicy, sweet and *ono*! Then there's pickled mango, green mango slices dipped in shoyu and vinegar sauce, mango bread, mango pie, mango chutney, mango ice cream...and on and on.

chanting of fire and light.

APRIL/APELILA

GOOD FRIDAY AND EASTER SUNDAY
Hawaii celebrates along with the rest of the world. Go to the Easter Sunrise Service at Punchbowl National Cementry for a real chicken-skin experience. No forget to set your alarm! And for the biggest Easter Egg Hunt in the Islands, be a part of the fun at the Manoa Campus of the University of Hawaii — last year they went for the Guinness Book of World Records!

MERRIE MONARCH FESTIVAL
A whole week of chicken-skin events, this one held each year in Hilo on the Big Island of Hawaii. Hula halaus (troupes) from just about every island compete for the title of best kahiko (ancient hula accompanied by chants) and best au'wana (modern hula accompanied by songs) halau, not to mention the wahine competition for Miss Hula Hawaii. And of course, in true Hawaiian style, there are a LOT of parties. A must-see in Hawaii — if you can get tickets! If not, it's still terrific to just be in Hilo during this exciting week. The festival is named for King David Kalakaua, the "Merrie Monarch" who is credited with a big part in the revival of the hula in modern times.

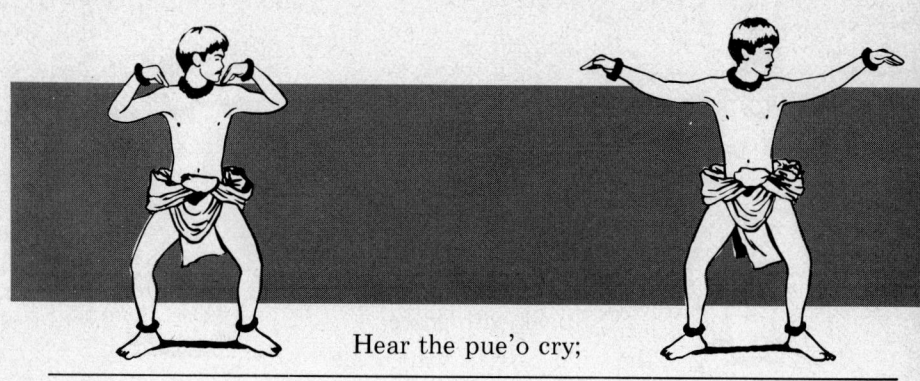

Hear the pue'o cry;

MARCH/MALAKI

3   GIRL'S DAY
Easy to remember — the third day of the third month. A Japanese tradition, and an example of how Hawaii's people love any reason for flowers and feeling special about others

17   ST. PATRICK'S DAY
Even in Hawaii, everybody wears green on St. Pat's Day — even if it's only a leaf. There's a genuine parade and, of course, plenty of action at the local pubs. Visit the Merchant Square at the beginning of Merchant Street in downtown Honolulu for an unreal time!

26   KUHIO DAY
State recognition of Prince Kuhio, a Hawaiian monarch. The keikis (kids) at Kuhio Elementary are especially proud their school carries his name and hold their own pageant in his honor.

CHERRY BLOSSOM FESTIVAL AND QUEEN
Sometimes held in April — a celebration of the Japanese community, filled with beautiful, quiet wahines. Well, quiet *sometimes.*

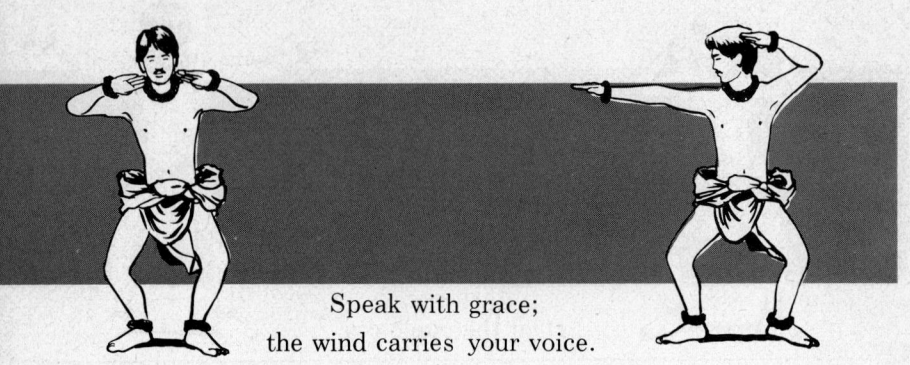

*Speak with grace;
the wind carries your voice.*

FEBRUARY/PEPELUALI

14 VALENTINE'S DAY
Leis and flowers for your favorite kumu (sweetheart). And no forget the chocolate-covered macadamia nuts!

CHINESE NEW YEAR'S DAY
If you forgot to celebrate the first time around, here's your second chance. The place to be is on Maunakea Street in Chinatown for goodies to eat, dragon dances, fireworks, and other cultural displays. Oh, and no miss the Narcissus Festival and Queen celebration if you like spahk all da pretty wahines!

Walk softly; heaven is in the earth.

JANUARY/IANUALI

NEW YEARS DAY
First chance to start the year off right. Recover from last night... clean up the mess the firecrackers left on the front lawn... put on the new clothes you got for Christmas. And if it's not raining, go to the beach!

20   Hawaii's legislators start their year off with Open House Day for the public. Morning sessions are held in House and Senate Chambers filled with flowers and leis from well-wishers, with plenty of local-style entertainment. This is one day legislators prepare not bills, but plenny kau-kau, and you get to see who's the best cook. Only in Hawaii this kine legislature!

To be sure that your Hawaiian vacation is everything you want it to be, we've included a calendar which lists many of the events and activities that happen here through the year. As we said in the beginning of this book, every ethnic group that has come to Hawaii has brought its own special gifts—and that includes a lot of celebrations and special events. These are part of the shared gifts of all cultures that make up our islands.

We've also included something extra: a Kahiko (ancient) Hula created especially for this book. Kahiko hula has recently experienced a revival in Hawaii. Hula was originally accompanied only by chants and the thumping of the *ipu* (ceremonial gourd), and was danced only by men. We chose this form to communicate our feelings about contemporary Hawaii and the special things that happen here. The hula begins with January and ends with December.

If you read the words of the chant and follow the movements of the hula, it will be satisfying and enjoyable for just what it is: a series of pictures and feelings about the land and people of Hawaii. But there's more there if you want to look for it: a deeper sense of what it means to be a part of Hawaii today, even if you're here only a few days or weeks.

This hula—and this book—came into being out of our desire to express our love and respect for Hawaii and its people, and to communicate that to the visitor. Please take it as an invitation to join us in our celebration. Aloha nui loa!

ROTTEN GUAVAS Usually found in forests in the mountains. Luckily your nose will tell you *before* you step on one!

KOREAN BARBECUE SAUCE This smell makes you so ono for kaukau. That means "hungry for food."

MOCHI CRUNCH Japanese munchies with characteristic smell.

GINGER Fragile yellow or white blossoms with a very sweet smell.

OCEAN The special smell that is one of the first to be missed by Island kids who go to any mainland school not on a seacoast.

ROTTING MANGOES Means mango season is pau. Everybody's too maxed out on mangoes to pick them off the tree, so they fall down on the ground and just stay there.

ADVANCE OF RAIN A special smell that's different in Hawaii than anywhere else.

BAGASSE (bah GAS) Hawaiian fuel source—leftovers from sugar cane.

BURNING SUGAR CANE Good kine pollution—makes bagasse. And sugar!

PAKALOLO Popular island smokes.

GARDENIA "Hawaiian rose" ... white, with heavy fragrance. Island favorite.

KIM CHEE BREATH How your breath smells after partaking of kim chee. Hard fo' get one kiss! (Also: Bagoong breath, Takuwan breath, Cuttlefish breath, Squid breath . . .)

MAUNAKEA STREET The smells of Chinese food and flower leis are pervasive on this street in downtown Honolulu.

PIKAKE (Pronounced PEA COCK AY) Jasmine. Small, white blossoms—very fragrant. A popular flower for leis.

TUNA PACKERS You know who these guys are as soon as they get on the bus. But ass why hard!

MOCK ORANGE Very common in Hawaii. Nice smell—and the bushes are good for playing hide-and-seek.

SULPHUR This smell means you're either near a volcano or you've discovered an Easter egg from last year.

DOLE PINEAPPLE CANNERY Not only can you see the big pineapple (when driving down Dillingham), you can also smell it!

ALA MOANA BEACH PARK BARBECUE On any weekend or holiday, you'll smell delicious charcoal-broiled ribs and teriyaki steak or chicken as families gather to "talk story" and "grind".

MAILE (rhymes with HIGHLY) A very special lei. Looks like a vine with different size leaves . . . and a sweet, subtle fragrance.

INCENSE We have all kinds in Hawaii—Buddhist . . . Hare Krishna . . . Pakalolo . . .

FISH MARKET Smell your way through Chinatown; go early to see the auctions.

Information to help prepare your nose for Hawaii.

instead of the hamburger.)

PUPUS (POO pooz) This is actually just the local word for "hors d'oeuvres"—anything you can eat that's not actually part of a meal. A good local bar serves plenty pupus.

PLATE LUNCH Hawaii State Meal. Two scoops rice, macaroni or potato salad, bed of lettuce or cabbage, and the main course.

SHOYU CHICKEN Chicken marinated in soy sauce (shoyu), then cooked in various ways.

SHAVE ICE Hawaiian version of "sno-cone." Sometimes with ice cream or azuki (ah ZOO key... sweet black bean paste) inside. Perfect on a hot day at the beach. Look for the shave ice truck.

HAOLE

Chances are you know Haole cuisine already. Just in case you don't, it includes things like BURGERS...STEAK AND POTATOES...FRIED CHICKEN...RIBS...SOUP AND SALAD...LOX AND BAGELS...and so on.

ONLY IN HAWAII!

A FUNNY T'ING HAPPENED ON DA WAY TO DA KITCHEN...

You'll encounter some foods that are found only in Hawaii but are not, strictly speaking, "Hawaiian" foods. Every ethnic group has brought their favorite dishes with them to Hawaii, and over the years many of them have grown and changed and become unique Island dishes. We've listed the most popular ones below.

SAIMIN (sigh MIN) Noodle soup with kamaboko, green onions, char siu. Both the Japanese and Chinese claim saimin has never existed in Japan or China.

HULI HULI CHICKEN "Huli" is Hawaiian for "turn over." This is chicken that's been broiled over charcoal, usually outdoors, and "huli'd" so it gets done on both sides.

LOCO-MOCO Unique local food with rice, hamburger patty, fried egg, and gravy on top. (Sometimes when you're not looking they throw in spam

FILIPINO

"DA P'INEST POOD IN DA ISLANDS!!"*

BAGOONG (bah gah ONG) Filipino fish sauce. Like hum ha, very strong.

LUMPIA (loom PEE ah) Filipino egg roll.

*unbiased Filipino opinion

PORK/CHICKEN ADOBO Pork or chicken prepared with vinegar, soy sauce and a little bit of sugar. Like Chinese sweet-sour dishes, but not quite as sweet.

PANCIT (PON sit) Filipino version of chop suey.

KOREAN

KAL BI (call BEE) Korean short ribs.

"DA BES'— AN' DA HOTTEST!!"*

KIM CHEE Cabbage, cucumber or turnips soaked in chili pepper sauce. HOT STUFF!

MAN DOO (mon DOO) Korean won ton — with hospital corners.

TAE GU (tie GOO) Cuttlefish that's been marinated in very hot sauce.

*unbiased Korean opinion

CHINESE

- **ALMOND PUDDING** White jello made from almond extract.
- **CHAR SIU** (char see OO) Cooked meat, colored red for good luck.
- **CHOP SUEY** Noodles, meat, vegetables, and anything else the cook wants to throw in.
- **CRACK SEED** Preserved fruit — sometimes pickled, sometimes salted, sometimes dried, sometimes the seed cracked into pieces. Chinese munchies.
- **DIM SUM** Chinese dumplings filled with meat, seafood and vegetables.
- **FORTUNE COOKIE** You know this one already.
- **FRIED RICE** Rice fried with meat, vegetables and seafood.
- **HUM HA** Chinese shrimp sauce. Very strong.
- **MANAPUA** Most popular kind of dim sum in Hawaii. Also called char siu bao (bao rhymes with "Ow!")
- **WON TON** Bite-size pupu. Meat wrapped in thin dough, fried, steamed, or put in soup.

*Unbiased Pake Opinion

JAPANESE

"YOU CANNOT COMPARE DA KINE! JAPANESE FOOD DA BES'!!" *

BENTO Box lunch, usually including rice, fishcake, pickled turnip (daikon), spam, shoyu chicken, teri beef, sesame seeds in the rice, and ume.

KAMABOKO (comma BO ko) Fishcake. Usually pink and white, or green and white. You'll see it in saimin, among other things.

MISO (ME so) Popular Japanese soup, made with soybean.

MOCHI (MOE chee) Soft little rice cookies.

MOCHI CRUNCH Rice Crackers.

MUSUBI (MOO soo bee) Rice balls (sometimes with ume inside).

SASHIMI (saw SHEE mee) Raw fish, sliced for maximum tenderness.

SUSHI (SOO shee) Japanese delicacy. Seafood or vegetables wrapped in rice. Comes in many shapes and sizes.

TEMPURA (tem POO dah) Vegetables or seafood dipped in batter and deep-fried.

TERIYAKI Japanese barbecue meat.

TOFU (TOE foo) White soybean curd; high in protein. Japanese staple.

UME (OO may) Pickled plum (usually red).

*Unbiased Japanee Opinion

PORTUGUESE

REMEMBER... OUR FOOD IS ONLY SECOND TO OUR CONVERSATION!*

BEAN SOUP Beans, onions, ham put together as only the Portuguese can.

MALASADAS (mah lah SAW dahz) Portuguese donuts — no hole. Delicious!

PAO DOCE (pronounced PAWN DULSS) Portuguese sweet bread.

PICKLED ONIONS Pickled Onions.

PORTUGUESE SAUSAGE Sausage made by portagees. Spicy!

*Unbiased Portagee Opinion

HAWAIIAN

'EY BRAH—HAWAIIAN GRINDS *NO KA OI*, YOU KNOW?*

CHICKEN LONG RICE Chicken cooked with long rice, which isn't rice at all but long, transparent noodles.

CHICKEN/SQUID LUAU Bite-size pieces of chicken or squid, with spinach, cooked in coconut milk.

HAUPIA (how PEE ah) Coconut pudding.

KALUA PIG Shredded, steamed pork, cooked in underground pit (imu).

KULOLO (koo LO lo) Taro pudding.

LAU LAU (rhymes with COW) Individual servings of meat and fish, wrapped in taro leaves and steamed.

LIMU (LEE moo) Seaweed. Better than it sounds.

LOMI SALMON Salmon mixed with tomatoes and onions, chilled overnight. This Hawaiian dish was actually invented by the whalers.

PIPIKAULA (pee pee COW lah *or* pee pee kah OO lah) Smoked meat.

POI (rhymes with BOY) Taro root, mashed into paste. Hawaiian staple food.

POKE (rhymes with OKAY) Hawaii seafood salad. WARNING: sometimes very hot and spicy!

*Unbiased Kanaka Opinion

MOLOKAI

MULE TRAIN RIDE Going down the steep cliff to Kalaupapa.

KALAUPAPA (Leper Colony) Remembering Father Damien and his dedication to and love for Kalaupapa's residents.

HALAWA VALLEY Seeing the blanket of green that covers it.

NIIHAU Seeing the "Forbidden Island" from the air.

WAIMEA CANYON Looking inside the "Grand Canyon of the Pacific."

KONA Picking coffee beans. Catching pigs in the mountains.

KAILUA BAY Watching the marlin and swordfish being weighed.

KEALAKEKUA BAY Seeing the Captain Cook Monument; knowing this is where he was killed.

KOHALA MOUNTAINS Driving through clouds and fog.

KAUAI

SLEEPING GIANT Seeing the rock formation that looks like a giant lying on his back.

MENEHUNE PONDS Seeing the ponds credited to Ipo's family.

MENEHUNE DITCH Ipo's family is said to have done this, too — in a single night!

BARKING SANDS BEACH Hearing the sand "bark" as you walk across it.

NA PALI CLIFFS TRAIL Emerging from the valleys and seeing the magnificent Na Pali (Hawaiian for "The Cliffs") and the deserted, inaccessible beaches. Watching the sun set here.

FERN GROTTO Getting married in this special place. Seeing it in Hollywood movies.

QUEEN VICTORIA Seeing the image in the rocks of the Queen sleeping peacefully.

LAHAINA ROADS Watching the whales pass through this channel between Maui, Lanai and Molokai.

KAANAPALI Playing on its beautiful beaches.

HANA Crossing the 52 bridges to get there. Experiencing its special beauty.

HASEGAWA GENERAL STORE Finding anything you need at this store in isolated Hana.

MAKENA Seeing a golf course with a heiau (Hawaiian Temple) on its grounds.

WAIANAPANAPA Remembering the legend of the princess who was killed by her husband in the cave, and knowing that once a year the water turns red.

LANAI

LANAI CITY Seeing the entire city at a glance. Feeling the peacefulness of this rural island.

BIG ISLAND (HAWAII)

MERRIE MONARCH FESTIVAL Seeing ancient hula performed. Seeing Hawaii's best hula dancers compete in a celebration of traditional dance. Feeling the excitement and energy of the crowds all over Hilo during this yearly event.

HILO Seeing fields of blooming orchids. Taking anthurium home with you. Parking downtown all day for 25¢, or seeing a movie for a quarter.

AKAKA FALLS Walking over the trail that encircles this Garden of Eden.

VOLCANO NATIONAL PARK Seeing lava trees along Devastation Trail. Smelling the sulfur smells from the lava vents. Seeing Halemaumau — the "fire pit."

VOLCANIC ERUPTION Being on the Big Island when this occurs, and seeing the red-hot lava shooting high into the air. Seeing a white owl in flight.

OHIA LEHUA Remembering that you must only pick this flower on your way home, or it will rain. Knowing it is Pele's flower.

KALAPANA Playing in its black sand.

PARKER RANCH Seeing acres of grazing land on the largest privately owned ranch in the U.S.

MANOA VALLEY Seeing the lush jungles in the back of the valley. Seeing the wisps of mist floating above the tops of the houses and knowing the Chinese call them "dragons." Seeing the many waterfalls that line the sides of the valley during rainy season.

WILLOWS RESTAURANT Eating wonderful food in the midst of flowers, trees and pools — and knowing you're right in the middle of high-rise Moiliili.

AIEA HEIGHTS Hiking near the heiau. Meeting the bear (!) who lives here.

THE KAMEHAMEHA SCHOOLS See Bernice Pauahi Bishop's gift to the youth of Hawaii. Looking for the wallabies that live above the grounds.

MOLOKAI CHANNEL RACE Watching from the cliffs of Diamond Head as the first canoes reach Oahu after crossing the channel from Molokai.

HAWAIIAN LANGUAGE Hearing it spoken.

MOUNTAIN MISTS On a clear day, looking toward the mountains and seeing the mists creeping down through the valleys.

MAUI

LAHAINA WHALING SPREE Imagining you were around during the days of whaling.

OHEO GULCH AND POOLS Playing in one of the Seven Sacred Pools or under one of the many waterfalls.

HALEAKALA Watching the sun rise from the lip of the crater. Looking down into the crater and feeling like you're on another planet. Playing in the snow.

SILVERSWORD Seeing this beautiful plant in Haleakala crater and knowing it grows nowhere else in the world.

MAUI ONIONS Tasting their sweet juices.

IAO NEEDLE Seeing this majestic rock rise up out of green, beautiful Iao Valley.

JOHN F. KENNEDY ROCK Seeing his profile in the cliffs.

LAHAINA TOWN Remembering the days when whalers caroused on its water front.

OLOWALU PETROGLYPHS Seeing and touching the ancient Hawaiian inscriptions.

PARADISE PARK Walking through the bamboo forest. Having your picture taken with a bird on your shoulder.

MANOA FALLS Hiking up to the falls past Paradise Park. Smelling flowers and plants you've never seen before.

POLYNESIAN CULTURAL CENTER Taking a one-day trip through Polynesia, all in one place. Seeing ancient hula. Seeing a coconut husked in just a few minutes.

SEA LIFE PARK Seeing a newborn baby seal. Watching a scuba diver pet a fish underwater. Watching dolphins play under the bright Hawaiian sun.

CASTLE PARK Going down the water slide.

FERNANDEZ FUN FACTORIES Playing the latest video games. Driving a bumper car.

KODAK HULA SHOW Smelling flower leis. Watching Hawaii's most popular symbol, a beautiful hula girl in swaying grass skirts.

QUEEN EMMA SUMMER PALACE Remembering the monarch who gave us Queen's Medical Center. Smelling ginger blossoms. Picturing the Queen riding horseback up to her palace.

ROYAL MAUSOLEUM Feeling love and respect for those who once ruled our land.

PALI LOOKOUT Viewing Kaneohe and Kailua — the windward side of Oahu — spread out in a magnificent panorama. Remembering the great battle won here by Kamehameha I. Driving into the mist that hugs the road. Seeing upside-down waterfalls. Feeling wind so strong you can actually lean back and let it support you.

MISSION HOUSES MUSEUM Seeing Honolulu as it once was. Remembering the missionaries' contributions to our culture and history.

BISHOP MUSEUM Feeling the love of the people Bernice Pauahi Bishop expressed when she gave them the land on which the Museum stands. Appreciating the dedication and time people give to help us remember and better understand our past.

UNIVERSITY OF HAWAII AT MANOA Experiencing one of the most beautiful campuses anywhere. Seeing students of all ages, races and cultures learning together.

LYON ARBORETUM Seeing plants and flowers that can't be found anywhere else on earth. Watching big Manoa raindrops bounce off the leaves.

PRINCESS KAIULANI HOTEL Remembering the beautiful estate which once stood here — Ainahau (EYE nah how) — where Princess Kaiulani lived. Remembering the peacocks that roamed the grounds.

SUNSET CATAMARAN CRUISE Cruising out of Kewalo Basin to the sounds of Hawaiian music and the smells and tastes of Hawaiian food. Watching sunset from the waters off Waikiki.

ROYAL HAWAIIAN HOTEL Seeing Hawaii's most famous hotel set like a pink jewel on Waikiki Beach. Experiencing its old-fashioned warmth and gentility.

FOSTER BOTANICAL GARDENS Smelling and seeing the profusion of different types of orchids. Seeing trees and plants from all over the world. Remembering that all this tropical lushness is right in the middle of a busy city.

HONOLULU ZOO Having a pigeon eat out of your hand. If you're from Hawaii, seeing a snake for the very first time. Becoming an adoptive parent to an animal.

HONOLULU AQUARIUM Seeing outrageously colored fish. Watching a seal tumble playfully in the water.

ROUND TOP AND TANTALUS Driving up the long, winding road through lush rain forests; seeing Honolulu spread out below. Smelling ginger in bloom, and guavas; hearing the clicking sounds the bamboo thickets make when the breeze blows through them.

CROUCHING LION Seeing the rock that looks like a crouching lion. Eating at the Crouching Lion Restaurant.

ALA MOANA BEACH PARK Jogging around it; playing volleyball; smelling barbecues as families gather for picnics and luaus.

CHINAMAN'S HAT Seeing this island off the Windward coast of Oahu. Seeing clearly how it got its name. Waiting for low tide so you can walk across the reef and visit the island.

KEAIWA HEIAU Walking on sacred ground. Feeling the strength of the *mana* (spirit) here.

DIAMOND HEAD Seeing it for the first time. Knowing it's part of an extinct volcanic chain. Hiking into the crater.

ALOHA TOWER Feeling the presence of the many visitors who have come to Hawaii on cruise ships. Remembering that this was once the tallest building in Honolulu!

KAWAIAHAO CHURCH Feeling the presence of Hawaiian monarchs who once worshipped here.

RABBIT ISLAND Remembering the hundreds of rabbits who once lived on this little island near Makapuu Point. Seeing the island as the head of a rabbit.

MAUNAKEA STREET Smelling Chinese food; visiting the many lei stands.

OPEN-AIR MARKETS Watching people barter. Smelling and seeing locally grown vegetables and fruits.

KAHUKU SUGAR MILL Seeing the history of the sugar cane industry in Hawaii. Shaking hands with a mongoose.

HONOLULU INTERNATIONAL AIRPORT Feeling the moist, warm air of Hawaii on your face for the first (or second or third) time. Receiving a flower lei and a kiss on the cheek.

BLOW HOLE Feeling the ocean spray on your face as you watch the column of water shoot up through the rocks. Feeling the rocks tremble with the power of the waves.

WAHIAWA PINEAPPLE STAND Tasting the fruit you've seen growing on the side of the road for miles. Learning that pineapples don't grow on trees.

WAIMEA FALLS PARK Jumping into the water above the falls. Seeing peacocks and remembering how Princess Kaiulani gave the jasmine flower its Hawaiian name, Pikake (pronounced PEA COCK AY). Seeing a coffee plant.

PEARL HARBOR TOUR Seeing the Arizona Memorial and remembering the attacks on Pearl Harbor; remembering those who gave their lives. Possibly remembering how it affected *your* life.

SENIOR CITIZEN CENTERS Feeling welcomed as Hawaii's kupuna (elders) share their feelings, stories, crafts, singing and dancing with you. Seeing history and tradition in their faces.

WAHIAWA Driving over airplane bridge.

HALEIWA
(pronounced HOLLY EVA) Eating shave ice. Feeling the "country" atmosphere of Oahu's North Shore.

HANAUMA BAY Knowing the ocean creatures here are protected. Snorkeling and seeing exotic tropical fish.

BYODO-IN TEMPLE Feeding the colorful Japanese koi (carp). Ringing the temple bell.

HALEIWA LANTERN FESTIVAL Watching the lanterns float out to sea on a warm summer night.

ALOHA WEEK PARADE Seeing brilliant floats covered with flowers. Watching the royal court pass by. Seeing the pa'u riders with their long trains almost reaching the ground.

ANNUAL UKULELE FESTIVAL Hearing the music of hundreds of strings together.

WINTER AT NORTH SHORE Watching the waves climb to 30 feet.

LOCAL PARTY Going to a local party for the first time and seeing all the shoes and slippers piled up outside the door.

LIQUID SUNSHINE Feeling warm raindrops while the sun is shining brightly. Noticing local people totally ignoring the rain, deciding you might as well do the same.

OAHU/HONOLULU Seeing it for the first time: a modern city set in the midst of green mountains and blue ocean.

STATE CAPITOL Seeing in it the joining of elements it represents: the volcanoes which gave us our land; the ocean that brought our people here; and the palm trees that supplied them with food and shade.

IOLANI PALACE Feeling the presence of the Hawaiian monarchs who called this home. Remembering the many celebrations held on the palace grounds.

KAMEHAMEHA STATUE Experiencing the strength and dignity of the warrior and chief who united our islands and became our King. On Kamehameha Day, seeing the statue draped with *long* flower leis.

HONOLULU HALE Our "Town Hall." Seeing the giant bird-of-paradise in bloom. Experiencing the warmth of its architecture.

OAHU

NEW YEAR'S EVE Hearing firecrackers all day, seeing fireworks at night, and anticipating the continuous roar of fireworks all over the city at midnight.

EASTER SUNRISE SERVICE AT PUNCHBOWL Watching the sunrise; experiencing the services.

UNIVERSITY OF HAWAII EASTER EGG HUNT Finding the last egg.

CAZIMERO BROTHERS MAY DAY CONCERT Plenty of chicken-skin at this special once-a-year concert under the stars (at the Waikiki Shell) by one of Hawaii's favorite musical groups.

MEMORIAL DAY SERVICE AT PUNCHBOWL Seeing the thousands of graves and the flags and flowers which mark them.

MANGO SEASON Picking the first mango. Experiencing the sweet, juicy taste. Stepping on the last mango of the season.

JAPANESE BON DANCE SEASON Remembering those who have passed away. Eating Okinawan donuts and teriyaki meat on a stick.

CHICKEN SKIN EXPERIENCES

Sunrise at Haleakala

"Chicken-Skin" is the Hawaiian version of "goose bumps." When you feel something very deeply, or you're moved, or you just feel good about something you're experiencing, that's chicken-skin. There are *lots* of these kinds of experiences in Hawaii, and on the following pages, we've listed some of our favorites. We wish you *plenny chicken-skin!*

For more specific information on any chicken-skin experiences listed here, you can:
   *Talk to your tour guide or the staff at your hotel;
   *Contact HVB (Hawaii Visitors Bureau);
   *Read one of the many tourist guides distributed throughout Waikiki;

WHAT? In pidgin, this often means "You like start somet'ing?" Often used with "Like beef?" or "Boddah you?"
"WHAT— LIKE BEEF?"

WHATEVAHS Whatever.

YEAH? Can be used at the end of almost any sentence in pidgin.

YOBO Korean person. Careful how you use this.

YOU This is an attention-getter. When you put it at the end of a phrase it means, "Yeah, you da one I talking to!" "No laugh, you!"

ZORIS (rhymes with STORIES) Slippers. Thongs.

TUTU (TOO too) Hawaiian grandmother.
    Plenny poi under da bridge.

U

ULE (OO lay) Boy's da kine.

USEDTATO Just like "used to," but locals put an extra "ta" in the middle.
    Haole: I've grown accustomed to your face..."
    Pidgin: "I getteen usedtato yo' face..."

USEDTATO

WYZ

WALA'AU (vollah OW) Talk too much.
    Diarrhea of the mouth.

WAHINE (wa HEE nay or va HEE nay) Girl or woman.
    What you see on the door of the ladies' room.

WHA'S DA HAPS What's happening?
    (Also **WODDASCOOPS?**)

T

TALK STORY Shoot the breeze. Often the reason for Hawaiian Time.

TALKING STORY

TALOFA (rhymes with SOFA) Samoan for "Howzit?"

T'ANKS EH? Pidgin for MAHALO.

TITA (rhymes with ANITA) Tough local wahine. Female version of MOKE.

TO DA MAX To the max. All the way.

TRY Pidgin for Please. "Try come!"

TRYING Pidgin for "You're trying too hard!"

22

SHAME No make shame or No be shame means "Don't be shy!"

SIDE Area.
    HAOLE: "We're from Boston."
    LOCAL: "Oh, east coast side, yeah?"

SLACK KEY Mainland guitars get tight strings — island strings are a little bit mo' relaxed.

SLY MONGOOSE One clevah buggah.

SMALL-KID TIME Childhood.

SPARK (pronounced SPOCK) To see, to check out. "Spark you laydah!"

STAY To be. Phone conversation:
    HAOLE: "Hello, is John there?"
    LOCAL: "Howzit. John stay?"

STINK-EYE Dirty look.

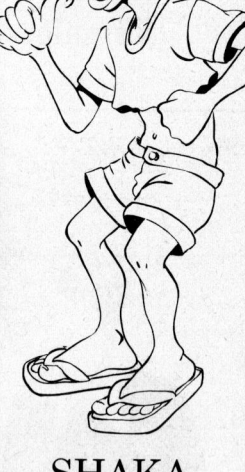

SHAKA

PAU (sounds like POW) Finished, done. Haole: "Are you finished eating?" Local: "You pau eat?"

PAU HANA (pow HA nah) Quitting time.

POPOLO (po POLO) Local boy — from Harlem.

PUKA (POO kah) Swiss cheese has lots of pukas.

PUPUS (POO pooz) Hawaiian for "snacks".

R

RADICAL Heavy duty. Extreme.

RIPPAH (REE pah) Ripper. Somebody who really tears it up.

ROACH, HAWAIIAN Bigger than the mainland kind. An' dey FLY!

S

SHAKA (shocka) Body language, local style. Means "right on!"

NO TALK STINK Don't say nasty things about people.

NOT! You're kidding! "Wow, you know Jennie hapai?" "NOT!"

O

OHANA (rhymes with DONNA) Family, or just like family.

OKOLE (rhymes with ROLY-POLY) What you sit on in Hawaii. This word does not mean "barstool."

ONO (oh no) Delicious. "Oh, da pupus was so ONO!"

O'WOT Or what. Often added on to the end of pidgin sentences. "Wow, you t'ink I dumb o'wot?"

P

PAKALOLO (pocka LOLO) Literally, "crazy weed." A few people in Hawaii smoke it.

PAKE (sounds like PARKAY without the "R") Chinese. Nevah like spend money.

NAH NAH NAH NAH NAH (rhymes with BAAA)
Just kidding.

NO ACT (NO AK)
  Stop showing off. Cool it.

NO CAN (no CAN) Cannot.

NO KA OI The best. Maui residents like to say "Maui no ka oi."

NO MO' None. A local does not say "I have none" — he says "I no mo'!"

MAKAI (rhymes with SKY)
Toward the ocean.

MAKE ASS (mek ASS)
To screw up; to make a fool of yourself. Also "Make A".

MALIHINI
(ma la HEENIE)
Newcomer to Hawaii.
What you find in tour buses.

MAUKA (mau rhymes with COW)
Toward the mountains.

MO' BETTAH Better.

MOKE (rhymes with COKE)
Local tough guy.

MOMONA (mo MO nah) Fat.

MUUMUU (MOO moo)
Hawaiian tent.

MUUMUU

LIKE BEEF? Wanna fight?

LOCAL Someone from Hawaii. (Don't call them "natives"!)

LOCAL STYLE The way people do things in Hawaii. Like: plenny leis at graduation time and birthdays; taking off your shoes before you go inside the house; spaghetti with 2 scoops rice; an' oddah kine stuffs li'dat.

LUA (LOO ah) Hawaiian bathroom.

LUAU FEET Big, flat feet.

M

MAHALO (mah HOLLOW) Hawaiian for "Thank you."

MAHU (mah HOO) Hawaiian for "gay".

MAINLAND Continental U.S.

KANE (sounds like CONNIE) Hawaiian for man. What you see on men's room door.

'KAY DEN Okay then! All right already!

KEIKI (KAY kee) Hawaiian for "small child". Rug rat.

KOKUA (ko KOO wah) Help. "Ey, we need yo' kokua!"

KOLOHE (ko LO hay) Rascal.

KONA WEATHER Hot and humid — when the trade winds stop and the wind blows from the south.

KULEANA (koo lay AH nah) Responsibility, job. Showing you the sights of Hawaii is your tour guide's kuleana.

KUPUNA (koo POO nah) Respected Hawaiian elder.

L

LANAI (la NYE) Porch or veranda.

LAYDAHS, LEDDAHS Laters. "See you later!"= "Laydahs, eh, brah?"

HOLOHOLO To go out and have fun.

HONEST KINE Honest? For real? *or* Yeah, for real!

HOWZIT You'll hear this a lot. It means "How ya doin'?"

I

I OWE YOU MONEY O' WOT? Pidgin for "How come you staring at me?"

J

JUNK Lousy, rotten. "Wow, dat movie was JUNK, yeah?"

JUNKS What girls have in their purse. What guys have in their car trunks. Also STUFFS.

K

KAHIKO (ka HEE ko) Ancient Hawaiian hula. Very popular in Hawaii today.
(See calendar in this book)

KAMABOKO SLIPPAHS (comma BO ko) Real thick slippers, thick like fishcake (kamaboko).

H

HANA HOU (ha na HO—rhymes with SNOW) Do it again! One more time!

HANAI (ha NYE) Adopted. There's a lot of this in Hawaii. That's why everybody is related.

HAOLE (Rhymes with "Now, Lee!") Caucasian.

HAPA-HAOLE (hop a haole) HAPA means half, so this is someone who's half Caucasian and half something else.

HAPAI (ha PIE) Pitter-patter of little feet coming soon.

HAWAIIAN TIME Late.

HELE ON (hey lay ON) Time to leave. "Let's hele on!"

F

FILIPINO (fillah PEE no) Local person who uses "P" in place of "F" (see page 42).

FRIENDLY ISLAND — MOLOKAI Small island, but big heart.

FUT How you spell "relief" in pidgin.

G

GARDEN ISLAND — KAUAI Greenest and wettest of the Hawaiian Islands.

GECKO Local lizard. Good luck to have inside the house. (Eats da roaches!)

GEEV'UM Go for it! "Geev'um, brah!"

GET Have. Haole: "I have a cold." Pidgin: "I get one cold."

GRIND To eat.

GRINDS What you eat when you grind. "Da grinds real ono ovah deah!"

DAT That.
Also LI'DAT (lah DAT) = like that.

E

E KOMO MAI (ay como MY) Come in. Welcome!

EH? Used for understanding and assurance. "T'anks, eh?" "You coming out tonight, eh?"

EWA (Pronounced like EVER without the "R") Direction. If you're in Waikiki, the opposite direction from Diamond Head.

C

CHO-CHO LIPS Thick lips.

COCKAROACH (KA ka roach) To steal or sneak away with.

COOL HEAD MAIN T'ING Relax!
HAOLE: "What did I just eat?"
TOUR GUIDE: "Jus' one small octopus. Relax. Cool head main t'ing."

D

DA The. Used in several ways.
(1) "Da breaks good today!" = "The waves are big today!" (2) "Oh, da cute!" = "Isn't that cute?" (3) "Oh, da hot!"="It's so hot!"

DA KINE (Literally, "the kind") Hawaiian mental telepathy. The phrase you use to say what you mean when you don't know what you mean (but everybody else does). Closest mainland equivalent: "whatchamacallit."
HAOLE: "Where's the whatchamacallit?"
LOCAL: "Wheah da da kine stay?"

BIG ISLAND Hawaii. The youngest and biggest Hawaiian Island — and it's still growing.

BODDAH YOU? Bother you? or What's it to you? If a local says this, it's a good time to leave.

BRAH Pidgin for pal or friend. "Ey, howzit brah?"

BROK' (pronounced like BROKE) Used to describe an intense experience. "Brok' da mout'" means "It's delicious."

BUGGAH Guy, friend. Also means pest. "Dat buggah! I going slap hees head!"

BUMBYE, BAMBAI By-and-by. The most exact measurement of time in pidgin.
    HAOLE: "When do we get to the Blow Hole?"
    LOCAL: "Bumbye."

A

-AH In pidgin, the sound that takes the place of "er."
    HAOLE: "George, where's your sister?"
    PIDGIN: "George, wheah stay yo' seestah?"

AKAMAI WAHINE

AKAMAI (AH kah my) Smart. Someone who knows the score.

ALOHA FRIDAY On Fridays in Hawaii, you wear an Aloha shirt to work.

ANY KINE Anything.
    HAOLE: "She'll say anything to get her way."
    PIDGIN: "She tell any kine fo' get her way."

B

BABY LUAU (LOO ow) Hawaiian bar mitzvah.

BENJO (BEN jo) Japanese word for BATHROOM See also LUA.

BENTO (BEN toe) Box lunch, Japanese style.

VISITOR'S GUIDE TO PIDGIN

HOWZIT! DIS SECTION OF DA BOOK DEDICATED TO YOU GUYS WHO NEVAH HEAR PIDGIN BEFO' AN' YOU LIKE FIND OUT WHAT US GUYS SAYING TO YOU LI' DAT! AN' YOU GOING *LAUGH* A LOT TOO, YEAH?

PIDGIN is what we call the special language we use in Hawaii to communicate with each other. Pidgin is not really that different from standard English, but it *sounds* a lot different. We've created a humorous guide to illustrate for you some of the more common Pidgin expressions so that you'll find it easier to communicate with local people.

But be careful! Pidgin is not a way of speaking that you just "pick up" in a few days! It's much more subtle and complex than that, because Pidgin reflects a whole way of thinking and an approach to life. You will notice, for example, that Pidgin inflections are very different from standard English. And that body language is more important. For those reasons, and many others, it won't work for you to try "throwing in" a couple of Pidgin expressions in your regular speech. You take a chance of offending the local people.

We really want you to use this guide first of all to *laugh,* and secondly to *listen*. With this small dose of local language, you'll find yourself better able to understand what's going on when you hear locals conversing in Pidgin. You'll begin to get a real sense of what it means to be local in Hawaii. We hope that this will make your stay in Hawaii that much more fun and meaningful, and that it will make it easier for you to really connect with local people, who are already very warm and open. So it is with great aloha that we extend to you this invitation to join us in enjoying Hawaiian Pidgin . . . brah!

KUMULIPO

Touch the land
and she will speak:
Of the gods alone
Of her birth from under the ocean
Of the creatures that were born to her

She will speak
Of the creatures born to the water
Of the creatures born to the sky
Of the coming of light

She will speak
Of man, and his birth
Of his love for the creatures
Of his journey across the water
From many lands far away

Of how he shared
So all could become one
Of the birth of a new language
So all could understand
Of the foods he brought
So all could eat

Of the heart of man
And his love of celebration
So all could sing
So all could dance
So all could feel

Touch the land
and she will speak.
This is Hawaii
This is she

A Contemporary Kumulipo

The Kumulipo is the sacred creation chant which allows a family of Hawaiian royalty (*ali'i*) to trace its roots back to the beginning of time. It brings power and prestige to their name and gives them right to be ruling chiefs.

Out of our respect and love for Hawaii and our desire to present you with a special gift, we have created a contemporary Kumulipo.

In order to do this, we first needed to acknowledge that what we were creating was not a Kumulipo in the true sense of the word, and that we had to surrender to powers greater than ourselves to create it.

Our creation chant speaks of Hawaii and how it came to be . . . of the birth of the land, plants, creatures and the coming together of cultures in this special place.

Please accept this gift with our aloha.

TABLE OF CONTENTS

A CONTEMPORARY KUMULIPO
(About Hawaii's creation) 4,5
VISITOR'S GUIDE TO HAWAIIAN PIDGIN
(A humorous guide to local talk) 7
CHICKEN-SKIN EXPERIENCES
(Special things and places to experience in Hawaii) 25
HAWAIIAN STEW or WHAT *WAS* THAT I JUST ATE?
(A guide to local foods)..................................... 37
SMELLS OF HAWAII
(A special section to help prepare your nose for Hawaii) 45
CALENDAR and CALENDAR HULA
(Only-in-Hawaii events, and a special Kahiko Hula) 49
ORDER BLANK/SUGGESTIONS 63

SPECIAL INSERT:

WAIKIKI AND OAHU MAPS (A colorful full-size map of Waikiki and Oahu, featuring bus routes, useful phone numbers, points of interest, etc.)

HOW TO USE THIS BOOK

HAWAII TO DA MAX is intended as a guide to the HEART of Hawaii. It's designed to let you know about Hawaii in a way that wasn't available before this book. HAWAII TO DA MAX is not a standard guide to Hawaii of the "Best Restaurants, Where to Rent a Car" variety. Instead, it's an animated, humorous look at what makes Hawaii special to those who LIVE here. It is our hope that HAWAII TO DA MAX will help make your stay in the Islands that much more memorable and enjoyable.

Use the PIDGIN DICTIONARY to learn how we talk in Hawaii — and what makes us laugh!

Use HAWAIIAN STEW (or What WAS That I Just Ate?) to heighten your appreciation of the great diversity of foods available in the Islands.

Use CHICKEN SKIN EXPERIENCES to find out about some special places and experiences loved by local people — many of them never before published.

Use the CALENDAR to get an idea of the many activities unique to Hawaii year-'round.

Use the WAIKIKI and OAHU MAP (insert) to find your way around. You'll also find bus routes, useful phone numbers and other information on the map.

There's lots more, too! SMELLS OF HAWAII ... A CONTEMPORARY KUMULIPO ... and a special KAHIKO HULA created just for this book (see the CALENDAR section).

WHAT *NOT* TO LOOK FOR:

As we said above, HAWAII TO DA MAX is not a standard where-to-go what-to-do guide to the Islands. It is intended to be used in conjunction with the many informational magazines and newspapers racked throughout Waikiki, such as THIS WEEK, GUIDE TO OAHU, SPOTLIGHT HAWAII, HAWAII ISLAND GUIDE, WAIKIKI BEACH PRESS, WHERE, OAHU DRIVE GUIDE, and so on. These publications are excellent sources of specifc information for planning your daily activities while in Hawaii.